Speaking Marks

Speaking Marks

◆

The stories, poetry, and prose of self-injurers

Kelly Underman

iUniverse, Inc.

New York Lincoln Shanghai

Speaking Marks
The stories, poetry, and prose of self-injurers

iUniverse books may be ordered through booksellers or by contacting:

iUniverse
2021 Pine Lake Road, Suite 100
Lincoln, NE 68512
www.iuniverse.com
1-800-Authors (1-800-288-4677)

ISBN-13: 978-0-595-35486-3 (pbk)
ISBN-13: 978-0-595-79978-7 (ebk)
ISBN-10: 0-595-35486-6 (pbk)
ISBN-10: 0-595-79978-7 (ebk)

Printed in the United States of America

Contents

Acknowledgements

I am extremely grateful to all those who submitted their works and shared their stories with me for this book. Without you, this would never have come to be. I am also grateful to the College Scholars Program of Case Western Reserve University for the guidance, inspiration, and support for this project. Thank you as well to the professors who guided and critiqued this work: Jonathan Sadowsky, Patricia Princehouse, Linda Ehrlich, Atwood Gaines, Deepak Sarma, and Laura Hengehold.

Introduction

What strikes me is how incredibly easy it was.

Easy? you will ask, noting that this book is about self-injury.

Yes, it was easy. An old, dear friend meeting me for a drink, the intervening years falling away. I claim I am in recovery, and yet I find myself, razor in hand, like the old days, measuring out the length on my skin, slicing with the precision of a diver.

It and I, the razor, we've lived out a passionate love affair, the kind worthy of Anaïs Nin. All that therapy, all that work, and putting together this collection brings to mind what it was like before all that. Before I began to use words and not marks on my skin to speak.

I came home from class, I took a shower, I took out my razors. I should have thrown them away but I did not. I found the perfect place. You always have to find the perfect place. You find the right spot, you fantasize about the length, the depth, the damage you want to do.

And then it happens. Everything else becomes remarkably quiet. It is like taking the phone off the hook, like unplugging my brain from my body like some phone cord tugged out of the wall.

It's second nature, you know, just to remember what it feels like again, to remind myself why I spent years trapped in this pattern, why so many of us find ourselves in love with causing pain. Pain to our own bodies, violating the body-world barrier and bleeding out everything. Making the marks talk.

And then after, I take out the butterfly bandages, the gauze. Second nature. Bandage up my thigh where I made this decision in incision.

I pad barefoot into the kitchen, pour a glass of red wine, smoke a cigarette, reflect. Haven't quite gotten my head reconnected. So I write this.

I have pages in front of me, the work and expressions of other self-injurers who are learning to make their voices speak instead of their marks.

What I have found is that no matter how hard you try, nothing else will speak like that cut or that burn or that bruise. No amount of poetry or painting can say what you want to say when you cut. You can attempt it, but often you fall so terribly short.

The literature on self-injury talks so much about secondary gain[1], about the rewards attention gives you. But often, I think, we self-injurers don't want attention as patients. We want you to sit up and listen, to hear what it is that speaks.

But we are stifled by cultural shame and guilt.

The secrecy and shame that keeps self-injury hidden is double-edged. It enables the self-injurer to hide, to indulge, in private, to not interfere in the lives of others. It also chokes the self-injurer. Once so deeply entrenched in that society, you do not rise easily into the light.

Self-injurers are afraid and ashamed in the face of others who do not self-injure. *They say they understand but they just don't* is the call of mourning. Many of us who self-injure are all too familiar with the look of shock, of horror, of confusion, on a loved one's face when at the point of confession. I know this look and I am tired to my bones of this look. The glance, the wanting-to-look-but-not-stare, when the scars are revealed. The brows knit together in worry, and the eyes dart away. The eyes are sad, clouded, unsure. The lips pulse as if to say, "Why?", but no words come.

However, more often than not, I have seen that look accompanied by something else: understanding. In my conversations with non-self-injurers, I have discovered that so many do understand, so many have felt the self-hatred that drives two percent[2] of us to self-injure.

In a conversation with a man I dated, he told me, I could have been there. "Skateboarding saved me."

I remember sighing, saying, I had nothing.

Sometimes I feel like the object of what could have been for some, if he or she hadn't found this, this, and this. I often wonder, am I defective for not finding something else?

Despite this understanding, these close calls with my reality, there is still a significant gap between what is experienced and what is understood by the outside. Those who do not will let their heads fall to the side and say, "Why do it?" And those who do have defiantly asked, "What's wrong with it?" When you are in the grip of a love affair with a razor blade, you exist in a parallel universe. There is a rift, a void, between you and those close to you. For them, black is black, and cutting is bad. For you, white is black, and cutting is your salvation.

---

1.   Secondary gain refers to the unconscious motivation to gain negative attention. Refer to Steven Levenkron's 1999 book *Cutting*, published by Norton, W. W. & Company, Inc.

2.   1400 out of 100,000 people self-injure, according to Karen Conterio and Wendy Lader's 1998 book *Bodily Harm*, published by Hyperion.

The goal of this book is to repair that gap. To meet the needs of both parties. Those who do not self-injure get a glimpse inside the world of the self-injurer. For self-injurers themselves, this book offers a chance to get out of the dark and into the light. To examine what has gone on for years in silence and shame out in the fresh air.

As the author and autobiographer of this book, I get the thrilling work of encouraging both ends together. I get to encourage self-injurers to step into the light. I also get to encourage anyone who has never self-injured to read their works and to understand.

Since my odyssey because at the age of fifteen, I feel like a veteran. I wear my scars and my hospital records like medals from an underground war. Self-injury is all around us in our culture. I imagine a jungle, thick with hiding spaces like some Vietnam movie, where rebels fight against oppressive forces without notice of a single civilian.

Fifteen is the age I footnote in my life and the average age of onset is around the teenage years[3]. This is perhaps the reason self-injury is seen as a teenage malady. In an article describing a movie featuring a thirteen year old who cuts, the author calls this a new fad.

Self-injury is the new anorexia. In a word: misunderstood.

From the stories circulating about self-injury, it's the new thing all the kidz are doin' in high school to elicit a sob and a shopping spree from the 'rents. Grrls with racoon-like eyeliner and black hair with the roots showing are listening to Lincoln Park[4] and breaking out the Bic razor.

Yes, I have met a few people matching that description, but abandon that image before venturing into the work presented here. Fads are Steve Madden heels, an Urban Outfitters belt, or perhaps one of those '80's inspired shirts at Delia*s. There is nothing faddish in the violent outcry of cutting the skin.

Let me interject here that cutting is a general term, although it is the most common method of self-injury. Burning is also pretty common, most notoriously with cigarettes. Hair-pulling and interfering with wound-healing are considered more mild forms. On the opposite side of the continuum, I know one young woman who has, in the past, deliberately broken her own bones. That and amputation are considered the most extreme methods.

---

3.   From Marilee Strong's 1998 book, *A Bright Red Scream*, published by Viking.
4.   Examples of songs (thanks to http://www.self-injury.net): Kittie's "Paperdoll", Papa Roach's "Last Resort", Eminem's "Stan", Linkin Park's "Part of Me" (which includes the line *New cuts cover where the old scars are*) and "Breaking the Habit", Slipknot's "Everything Ends", and so forth.

Nor is self-injury limited to females. Males are also afflicted, but perhaps not at the same rate. The acts of self-injury are violent and violence is traditionally associated with masculinity. Boys in our society are steered to more self-abusive sports and activities, such as skateboarding, football, and other extreme sports.

I mentioned the man I dated who found skateboarding instead. Another friend and lover of mine recounts using football as a means of escape. When I would discuss my scars and impulses, he would tell me, I never did that but I used to play until I saw spots.

Granted, a wound sustained from fumbling a rail slide via skateboard is much more acceptable than a wound created from your own hand holding a hammer.

Then again, madness is a woman's domain[5].

But on the other hand, self-injury isn't really madness. (When you have been cutting yourself in secret for years, you will get used to this eternal internal tug-of-war between feeling crazy and feeling sane.)

I had my first knowledge of self-inflicting injuries as demon possession. In Mark Chapter 5, Jesus casts the demons ("legions" of demons, actually) out of a man who beats himself with rocks. This staunch, insanity-is-evil view permeates popular views of self-injury. The act of defiling the flesh with marks smacks of medieval madness.

In my conversations with self-injurers, there are those who ask, quizzical, Why not self-injure?

Self-injurers are, according to the clinical literature, generally people who have lived through trauma. The majority of people with this behavior are victims of sexual violence, abuse, or both. There is a high comorbidity, or co-occurrence, with eating disorders. Much of my early experience with other self-injurers was via an eating disorder support forum run by a close friend.

Coming out of these experiences, the human mind often dissociates. In her book *The Myth of Sanity*, Martha Stout explains how dissociation is an adaptive technique the brain uses. Theories suggest that this form of adaptation preserves the brain, a sort of cognitive self-defense. This is familiar to most people without much experience studying psychology as so-called multiple personalities, or dissociative identity disorder, as it is called now.

Studies of self-injury suggest that this behavior develops similarly to dissociation. It is a protective strategy that a person will engage in to keep safe from over-

---

5.   As a feminist and mental health activist, I have read extensively on the societal link between women and madness. For more information, I recommend *The Gender Gap in Psychotherapy* by Elaine Carmen, et al, and *Women's Madness* by Jane Ussher.

whelming emotion. The simplest way to explain my cutting, I have found, is that when overwhelmed with confusing emotions, it was just easier to point to a cut and say, There, I know that hurts.

Interestingly, self-injury is also a way of dealing with dissociation. You are probably familiar with this. When performing a common activity, your brain may drift out into what my sixth grade teacher loved to call La La Land. This is actually a common form of dissociation. Then when you actually burn yourself on the frying pan or get bitten by a horsefly, you snap back into yourself. For self-injurers, the act of inflicting pain functions as a convenient way to feel something, to feel anything.

I have heard self-injurers say that cutting is the only way to know the body is still alive. I think that's why eating disorders and self-injury have a high comorbidity: disconnection with the body. I have spent much of my life feeling like my brain isn't plugged into my body properly, like I came from the factory improperly assembled.

Pain is the best way to reconnect with the body, I have found. No other experience will bring you as sharply back to your flesh and bones as pain. Drugs and alcohol only further the disconnection. Sex is an entirely different matter, an activity deeply tied to fantasy and escape. I ran for a number of years, until my knees became painful at eighteen, and I found that the best run was when I could leave my body to its working and escape into thought.

With this laid out, I feel I can more properly explain how self-injury is not a suicidal gesture. Sitting in that ER for my five stitches when I was nineteen, I told countless doctor who have all faded into one white-coated faceless blur that I was not suicidal. Even though I had cut deeply enough to require immediate medical attention, I had no interest in kicking the bucket.

Aye, there's the rub: I was interested enough in the business of living that I cut.

Without cutting, I probably would have been so overwhelmed with emotion that a suicide attempt may have occurred. A dear friend of mine, during a dark phase in her life, told me that she had two things keeping her alive: purging and cutting.

For the reasons I have explained, self-injury is a damned good way to keep the self sane enough to keep on living. In fact, recent developments in therapy for self-injurers have therapists acknowledging what a great tool it is for survival[6].

---

6.   This therapy is known as dialectical behavior therapy.

To be perfectly honest, there are moments in my life when I am overcome with the realization that my only solution is to cut. Nothing, nothing, nothing will ever make me feel as good and calm and okay as cutting will. This is what is so difficult to explain to those close to me. An act so mired in shame and secrecy for me also holds the magical key to making everything feel All Right.

And to be even more honest, I do not know the response to that feeling. When I was asked, Why not cut?, I was dumbfounded. There was no answer for me to give, besides the usual, worn out story about the ER experience. I am sick of recounting that and how I could have died from shock, blah blah blah ad nauseum, as a reason to not cut. That is a reason for me to question the experience of self-injury in culture, but not a reason not to cut.

As you will read in this book, we all find our own peace with self-injury. It is an entity we find a way to co-exist with.

No, I did not find an alternative to cutting myself or putting cigarettes out on my forearm. I was not saved by extreme sports or a really great therapist. I don't even think I was saved. I carry around on my body a story in scars that tells everyone how not all right I used to be and to an extent still am.

I still wear long sleeves. I have found this peace of mind when dealing with loved ones, with those who scan my arms like a barcode, hoping not to turn up a new blip of sadness.

The truth is, I am angry. I am fucking angry and I haven't spent hours upon hours in therapy to not embrace my rage. And after receiving the works I did while compiling this book, I realized that I am not alone. A lot of us are pretty jaded.

I, for one, feel left behind by society. If the cause of my scars had been a physical illness or operation, then I would be permitted to bare my skin. If what was wrong with me had been in my body and not in my head, then perhaps I would have gotten care covered by my insurance.

For the most part, I am jaded that my society has fostered and then rejected the behavior I love and loathe. Of all the conflicting messages in culture today, those toward self-injurers are the most insidious. I am tired of watching my friends and lovers split into two halves. I am tired of society ignoring the marks that speak so loudly.

WHAT IT'S ABOUT

Michelle P.

It's about the anger,
It's about the hate.
It is why I hurt.
It's why I mutilate.
It's about unanswered love,
It's about trying to self-assure.
It's why I am so fucked up,
It's why I self-injure.
It's about the way you hug me,
although you'll never be mine.
It's how you're the only one
that knows when I'm not fine.
It's about how we can talk,
Till early in the morn.
And how you know to comfort me
when I feel forlorn.
It's about feelings,
neither of us can change.
Though our feelings are different,
and sometimes they range.
It's okay not to love me,
It doesn't hurt too much.
It's about me letting go;
It's about the heart you clutch.
It's about how you can not stop me,
It's about my blades on the shelf.

Don't think you could ever end
What I'm doing to myself.

CRIMSON KISSES

Auna Joslyn

A climb to the summit
Is met with a storm
A wave from a blade
A crimson kiss, warm

Each slice makes me tremble
Cry out in my pain
But I keep on going
To reach that one plain

I hear you calling out
For me to not fall
To stop and be healed
Yet I will not surrender my all

This river of crimson
Flows out before me
I swim to the surface
To set myself free

Slowly I sink
Drowning in strife
I gasp out for air
But become one with the knife

A moment, a swipe
And a red line takes place
A smile of release wipes
The tears from my face

I know I am drowning
No matter how hard I climb

The summit grows taller
I fear for my time

I don't wish to kill
But to simply release
The darkness inside me
That's tearing me piece by piece

I know it returns
It always does and will
Yet I go back for more
Of my deep, stinging thrill

The night winds to soothe me
The stars watch me sleep
A smirk to the heavens
At the sin that I keep

A secret that no one
But me and some know
For a dark type of healing
A spirit to grow

To bask in a world
Of an undying, dark bliss
I reach for the solace
Of a sweet, crimson kiss...

HAD TO FULFILL THE DREAM

Amanda Smith

Had to fulfill the dream
Cut wide open across the lines
Ill with misunderstanding and guilt
Suffocate with no-one around to hear the cries
Drown it out with blood
Hope to fall to death in dreams tonight
Scared of life and scarred forever
No reason to carry on without you
Can't be what would've made us
Us

A RAZOR BLADE

Lucy DeLaurentis

A single sheet of hatred,
So thin,
Causes so much bleeding.
No one knows how much.

Her scars
Break
His heart,
His heart's been
Smashed before, but
Not in the same way.

Everyone thinks she's suicidal.
She's never wanted to die.
And it's so strange
How
A single sheet of hatred
Causes so much bleeding…
And no one knows how much.

A MOTHER'S LOVE

Amanda Bruner

You taught me to be who I am
And then berate me for who I've become
What did I do to deserve all this, Mom?
To this pain I'm about to succumb,

I'm sorry I can't be great
Or even just good enough for you
Nothing I do is correct or okay
There's nothing left for me to do

I cry every night
Wishing I was all right
And good enough for your love

I watch you love both of them
Hug both her and then him
Then scream at me
For the tiniest of things

What can I do
To be good enough for you?
To earn the love that my mother should feel...

A WHISPER

Rufus Graham

A whisper to a scream
A drop to a river
I release my pain
As I quiver

Letting go of everything
I feel free
For the first time in my life
I can see

With one last breath
I say goodbye to my life
All I do now
Is remove the knife.

ADDICTIONS

Nicole Fillmchuk

One obsession
Uses repression.
A ruthless attempt
To acquire progression.

One inspection
Of a reflection.
Reveals a failure
In a strive for perfection.

One mentality
Contains brutality.
An imperceptible
Borderline personality.

One perception
A misconception.
Might appear to be
A self-deception.

One sensation
Presents frustration.
Only one way out-
Dissociation.

Some afflictions
Caused by restrictions.
There is no way out
Of my addictions.

MY STORY

Miss Collier

I'm in 8th grade. I just got suspended from a school dance for drinking with a friend prior to the activity. The principle said that I'd be gone for five days. During those five days, I don't think that I talked to anyone that week besides my mom and my sister.

I remember that it was around Christmas time and I was sitting by the tree snooping through presents when suddenly it hit me. I was going to be behind on my homework, all of the parents are going to hate me, and I was going to have no friends. Out of rage and anguish, I took one of the glass balls hanging from the tree and threw it against the wall.

I hurried over to the mess and started picking up the pieces when, out of nowhere, I cut my finger. I picked out a sharp-looking piece and dragged it across my wrist. It was almost an out of body experience. I didn't feel it, I just watched and suddenly I felt a wave of relief. All of my troubles and fears had been washed away. Almost immediately, I started slicing up my wrists. I wiped the blood on a piece of paper and kept it for a while. Why did I do that? I have no clue, but I felt so much better.

After that first encounter, I thought nothing of it. I only did it once. There was no way in hell that I was or ever would be a self-injurer. A few weeks went by and I was fine.

A few months went by only to lead up to my second and last suspension. This time, it was for pot. It was caused by my mom. She searched my room and found notes from the guy who sold it to me and a roach. She told the principal. The day after that, I walked into school only to have my friends and peers scream "NARK" at me.

I had finally had it. I went home and cut again. I showed my mom the cuts and told her that it was because of her. She threatened to take me to the hospital but I somehow talked her out of it. That was possibly one of our biggest mistakes.

After that, I maybe self-injured once a month up until that next summer. However, I still wasn't classified as a self-injurer. I never thought of it that way, it was only something to relieve myself. To me, cutting is/was like a drug. It puts me in a different place, gives me a high that I can't describe. It made me feel whole, peaceful, and happy for a minute or two. That's all I needed.

The summer prior to my sophomore year, my mom, step dad, brother, sister, my sister's friend, my friend, and myself went on a trip to an amusement park.

The day that we were scheduled to leave, my mom and step dad got in a huge fight in front of everyone. I was humiliated, livid, and depressed. I left the room, selfishly leaving my friend in there and meandered around the hotel. I avoided all of the guys that I met the previous night because I knew that my mom would come looking for me and embarrass me by yelling at me or doing something obscene. She did just what I thought what she would do.

On the way back home, I sat in the front seat and buried myself under a blanket with a dull razorblade in my right hand and cried as I started viciously making slits amongst my left arm. When I got home, I came to the conclusion that I had nothing to live for and I took every sleeping pill that we had. Unfortunately, I woke up the next morning. I was very sick and unable to go to work.

I guess that since that weekend, I've been a regular cutter. Sometimes I go through periods where I do it every day for a few weeks and then there are times where I'll go a few weeks without. I think that a lot of people know about my issue with the razorblade. My friends have never said anything though besides, "Do it again and I'll kick your ass." I think that they either don't care or they don't take it seriously.

I am thankful, though, for my boyfriend who has been there by my side ever since he found out about it. He is one of the few people who hasn't judged me or ridiculed me because of a problem, an addiction that I can't seem to put a permanent stop to. For that, I'm very grateful.

A major downside to my problem is that every time I look down at my arms, I just feel ashamed. Ashamed of what I've done to my body, to myself. It's the exact same feeling when I look at my legs and my stomach.

I also get the pleasure of having people ask, "Why do you have so many scars on your arm?", "What are those big one's from?" I never have the right answer for them either, I'm not out to please people otherwise I wouldn't self-injure in the first place.

I've been a self-injurer for almost five years. I don't know how long I've been like I'm proud of it because I'm not. The memory of my first encounter just sticks out in my mind so vividly. I think that's why most people who self-injure know how long it's been. Right now, it's been about a month give or take since I last cut. I'm just waiting for something to set me off.

ALONE

Shari Taylor

I am all alone…
I am bleeding
I am SCREAMING
but I can't let it out
I want to sleep forever
I don't want to do this anymore…
everything is crashing to the ground now
The lovely temple I built
that I thought would never fall
it was made of paper
and he blew it all down.

WHAT CAN YOU DO?

Jenna Perkins

What can you do?
When people hurt you?
What can you say?
To those who betray?

Turn away and hide
Just pretend you tried
Run to your tiny room
Your hollow tomb

Take out the blade
Let it be your aide
In taking away the pain
Your silent bane

The crimson flows
Away your pain goes
The crimson stripes
The mindless swipes

Lay back and breathe
Let your blood seethe
The pain released
The aching ceased

BEYOND

Jillian Allen

Alone and/Without
Collapsing in desperation
I fall to my knees
Trembling
As the cold metal Blade/Tears into my skin
Release,
Silence,
And then,
Emptiness
Once Again…
For only God
Can save me now

BLOOD

Michelle P.

Blood's the tears that I can't cry.
Blood's the sad look in my eye.
Blood's the reason I exist.
Blood's the excuse for that kiss.
Blood is why I never scream.
Blood's what haunts me in my dreams.
Blood's what's going to let me die,
but blood's also why I'm alive.

LIQUID SCREAM

Alicia Noecker

That horrible dark searing hole
Seems to be rising
Such seeping pain
From the finger nails to my lips
A liquid screaming
She finds it hard to lay awake.

CONUNDRUM

Malea

I fill my life with little things…
Television Shows.
Jobs.
Tattoos.
Pets.

Where are all the Big Things?
Real Friends.
Careers.
Love.
Children.

All these little things take over till I have no room for the big.

Like a jar filled with sand, once it's full, there's no room for hidden
   treasures.

The Sand is overwhelming.
QuickSand.
The more I try to free myself of it, the more it holds me fast.

It fills my eyes, my ears, my nose, my lungs…
It chokes me.
I cannot breathe.

CRIMSON KISSES

Susan Pepperman

Crimson kisses across my body
Across my abandoned soul
Many a lonely nights
Are spent with me and my filled up bowl

No one can understand
The pain I always endure
The only quality time I spend
Is with me and my razor

Crimson kisses are placed on my leg
No one seems to care
I keep it hidden from the whole world
For only myself has to bare

I kiss myself all the time
There is no other way
I lick all the crimson off of my body
It is my favorite time of day.

COLD

Crystal

It's cold
Numbness sets in
Nothing
Silence
Pain now takes over
Breathing is not an option
Blurred vision
What is there to see
There it lays
A million pieces
All for you
Look what you did
Don't fix it, you can't
Its bitter and sharp

TRAPPED INSIDE

Cat Munroe

Empty threats
Hollow lies
This is something I despise

Pulsing tears
Blood stained eyes
My happiness is a mere disguise

Glimmering blades
Broken skin
Pardon me for sounding grim

Saddened waves
Blood choked sin
Someone let my baggage in

Drowned in tears
blood entwined
Help me get out of my mind

Meaningless sentiment
Unspeakable dread
it is death that I tread

Endless horror
Unspeakable gain
But it's from this I must abstain

So will I win
Or will I lose?
It is myself that I abuse

DEAD JELLY FISH

Joti Whited

i was walking along the beach
when i found a secret treasure
it was only a dead jelly fish
but it was grand beyond measure

the urge to touch it was so overwhelming
i had to be restrained
it was so shiny and pink
my excitement could barely be contained

so instead i took a mental picture
for me to always remember
never to leave my jelly fish on the beach
for others to dismember

i was talking to a friend
when i let a little secret slip
her mouth gaped open like a dead fish
she didn't look like she could keep it
but her compassion was in her kiss
as she fought to contain it

i had this urge to slap her pretty face
i could barely restrain myself
and my face bloomed pink with shame
my secrets kept on that shelf
should have never been given a name

so we laughed and took a picture
to display on the wall in the hall

to remember our day of fun
that wasn't any fun at all.

i was stalking this pretty girl
when suddenly she turned around
her mouth turned down with a sad little frown
and i could tell just from the sound of her rapid breathing
that she hadn't wanted to be found.

i had this urge to run up to her
i had to look away to restrain myself
from wrapping my arms around her tiny little waist
to slide my tongue across her lips
and see how they would taste

instead i snapped a picture
for me to remember just the way that she looked
from her hazel green eyes
to her pretty little thighs
on that day i fell in love with a girl.

i'm looking in the mirror
at the remains of a little girl
nothing left but a dead jelly fish
waiting for that one last kiss
to release her from this world.

THE SOLDIER

Morgan Anne Wulforst

Torn, beaten, battered.
Boot soles worn smooth,
Like the cloth woven
From and unwinding
Cigarette bobbin.
The heavy, definitive

Loom of tainted
Life produces monochrome
Canvas, dyed tn the

Pool of bloody tears,
Cried by our melted souls.
Time's finger's stroke the canvas,

Allowing it to become knapped
Velvet, studded with glittering
Dreams of the dead.

Gazed upon by
The solarity of
The living innocent,

The crackling
Black of the lucent
Flare overwhelms the

Still of the
Choking surround.
Whenever shall I

Be allowed to fold,
Fold inwards and
Die?

Gored by the spindles
Of a spiteful country's
Faded war, I am
One step closer
To perfection.

DEALING

Malea

Should it scare me that I want to cut?
It's just that everything right now is so fucked up.

I don't know what to feel
What to say
How to act
What to do

This is harder than anything I've ever been through
If only I could feel it, I could deal with it.

But I can't feel.

Take the lighter, watch it burn,
1 minute, 2 minutes, 3 minutes...
There, that should be good.
Press it against my skin.
Can I feel it?
Just barely, I'm mostly numb.
It's cool now.
Let's try again...

Open the tool kit, there's a box knife in there
Slide it across, come on now, put some pressure behind it,
Watch the beads of blood appear...

Not deep enough to harm,
Just deep enough to feel.

What's next?

I
Still
Feel
Empty…

SILENT MOURNER

Aly

she reaches out
but no one is there
she cries desperately for help
but all she will find is despair

her world has been abandoned
everyone has fled
from the unavoidable dishevelment
stored up in her head

the only sound
comes from a corner
the pouring of blood
the tears of a mourner

the scarlet red liquid
that pours from the lines
are the pains that she feels
the pains of all kinds

the girl does not weep
for her lines do it for her
the red puffy marks
that forever adorn her

her world is not dark
but it's getting there
the flowers will soon wilt
leaving the land unwelcomely bare

with the flowers now gone
the girl has no hope

she no longer wishes to live
in a place where she can't cope

just as the land
becomes barren and dark
there is a bright light
a vibrant spark

it seems to engulf her
and diminish her fears
it almost enlightens her
and halts her red tears

what is that light
the shining bright star
the one thread of happiness
that won't leave a scar

day by day she seems to grow
stronger and more alive
she is lifted of all burdens
given what she had so been deprived

as the time goes on however
there seems to be something wrong with her light
it is starting to dwindle
and is no longer so bright

the girl knew what was happening
all too well
the happiness she was feeling
would soon be replaced by her hell

she quickly awoke
from her tranquil dream

reunited with her nightmare
her world had lost its gleam

it was too good to be true
she knew that without a doubt
she was doomed for a lifetime
and there was no easy way out

why did she do it
why did she dream
she brought back her hopes
when things were not what they seemed

with this piercing recognition
she crawled back into her corner
took out her weeping blade
and once again became a silent mourner.

DEAR RAZOR

Anna Bray-Roe

Sorry Razor, you've been replaced
I found a more sufficient blade
One that slices through the skin
Releases blood from deep within

All those lonely nights I cried
From all the pain and hurt inside

You were my friend for some time
But now that I have crossed the line
I've made a friend named Butcher Knife
There's a chance, someday, he'll take my life

That's a chance I'll have to take
To get me through life's big mistake

Don't worry, Razor, I'll think of you
Knowing that you got me through
Those first two months when it wasn't so bad
Before life had driven me mad

But life's too hard for such a small friend
Butcher Knife will see me through the end.

FATHER, DAUGHTER

Amber Hodge

You use little excuses
To cover up my pain
"It's just the teenage years
I went through the same"
I'm smarter than to believe something like that
I can feel it in my heart
But you'll believe what you want to
You've done that from the start
You cover up the fact that
I have a disease
It eats away at my spirit
But you'll believe what you want to
You just hide your eyes from seeing it
You tell your friends,
"Kids just don't know what pain can be"
But you'll believe what you want to
Just cover your ears from me
I've tried to open up to you
But you were engulfed in playing your 'game'
But you'll believe what you want to
And try to force me to think the same.

SET TO SLAY

Alicia Noecker

I'll let you march through
And slay my insides
Draining each blush of blood
Each wisp of breath
Upon your weapons
Your sour tainted tongue
A hand of power
Lay loosely
By the pen
Velvet black leaked through
The pointed twisting ending
Twining to meet ends.

SCAR ME BEAUTIFUL

Christi Wilmoth

The pain of it is wonderful
It flows from the inside
The point caressing my soul
So much joy I can't take it
As it flows and streams along
I stare into the empty space
That I am leaving behind
Suddenly I feel content
Because that empty space
Has been filled

IN YOUR HOUSE

Jodie R. Fox

I am afraid
Afraid of the way curtains dangle
hanging by their necks
afraid of the helpless gray carpet
laying impotent with defeat
the bare Chrismas tree
with its clouds of tinsel trying to fatten naked gaps
afraid of the heavy wooden TV
the lack of a fireplace
afraid of how the four o'clock sun obtrudes
ungratefully into the dusty living room
just before you get home
I fear the pea colored couch
your prickly beard
your eyes laughing
lips
mouth
stained yellow teeth
your breath
my head on the bathroom floor
I fear the coolness of pink tiles
so tiny and close together
your finger sticking callously
in my ear
my warm mouth
my too many places
I fear to taste vomit
I fear the smell of chicken soup polluting the kitchen air
I fear the linger of a silence

so loud it keeps me awake nights
I fear footsteps above
but in the quiet I make myself bloody again
Because I am afraid
Afraid of becoming
one of your cigarettes.

NICOLE FILLMCHUK

Repressed Mutiny

I'm still here.
I haven't gone anywhere.
Don't bother to fear.
When I'm done, your mask will still be there.
It's my turn—
Just to remind you you're not sleeping.
I'm starting to burn,
And soon I'll explode and send you weeping.

I want to remind you that I'm real—
The void that you ignore.
When you cry I take my chance to steal.
I take everything worth living for.
I'm your pain,
And when I'm done I'll go back inside.
You're only sane,
Because I let you put me away to hide.

I'm the side that no one sees—
They wouldn't comprehend.
When you're alone you can listen to my pleas.
The other times are just pretend.
I'm every tear you shed,
And every searing pain in your heart.
As you lay here on your bed,
I'm tearing your world apart.

It's my turn for a while—
A reminder of what you ignore.
Then you can put on your smile,

Just as you've done before.
But now I'm taking my chance,
To show you just how much you ache.
Then you can go back into your trance,
And become the you that's fake.

No one knows you carry me—
There's nothing they can do.
Alone forever you will be,
With me lurking inside of you.

FEELINGS

Jamie-Lee Hayhurst

Feelings are spinning out of control
Just like empty bottles beginning to twirl
Emotions are wary, people are scary
Blood is like water, the stinging sensation
Like the wind on a cold night
It makes such a noise, such a pain
Nobody else knows, unless you are one
Someone who is like us doesn't judge, just helps
We all cry the same, just in different ways
Some turn to drugs, liquor or sex
Others turn to hurting themselves instead
Nobody's the same, they never will be
Unless you try and stop us, we'll never change
Everybody judges, tells us we're seeking attention
Oh are we? We're not. We don't like it, we hate it
Just about as much as BUSH hates gays.
He doesn't want it, like we don't, but we get it, like he does
We try not to brag, but when we do show, you all get so mad
You say that it's bad, we know that already
Just please don't tell me, "don't do that anymore"
I know and I try, but it's so hard inside
To turn off that voice that tells me what to do
I'm sure you don't have one, or maybe you do too
A down whirl spiral of emotions and thoughts
We're not very good at coping with things,
But if you gave us a razor, a needle or blade
We could draw you a map, on our fresh skin
Of how we feel and what we go through
Help stop our emotions from running away,

All the time is a struggle, each and every day
To not go too deep, or even hit a vein
You have no idea of our pain
We let ourselves endure
Or maybe you do, 'cause you do it too
By drinking or tripping out, or giving yourself away
Because we're all the same. In each and every way.

WEAKENED

Mercedes

"...And with drying tears streaking down my face, I'm reminded just how pretty the blood is—but I have weakened. The cuts are nothing compared to before, will I ever be there again? Now that I've given in am committed to this path or is this just a one time thing? Is this because he left—will it change when he gets back? Or is this just me...more free and allowed to be me?"

REFUSE

Amy Rowland

you watch me bleed
yet you refuse to
to bandage me
you watch me cry
but still refuse
to comfort me
you watch me smile
but you refuse
to see past all my fakeness
you watch me hurt
yet you refuse
to help me heal
you watch me fight
but still refuse
to free me
you watch me die
yet you refuse
to change.

MY IMPERFECT SOLITUDE

Anonymous

Haunted by my loneliness,
I am forever alone
My heart is torn and severed
My soul bruised and broken
I'm dying inside
Tears are all I have
Pain is all I feel

I'm sitting here in a dark bathroom
Blade in hand
Staring into my solitude
Pain-filled regrets clouding my mind,
Shown through the scars imprinted on my body
And yet again,
My past continues to play
Like a broken record
Skipping over and over again

Silent tears flood my eyes
And fall onto my pale cheeks
I cry out to God
Please forgive me
I'm so lost
My bleeding soul's about to fall…

Sink the blade into my flesh
This familiar crimson river appears,
All the hurt and misery
Bleeding and pouring out of me
And for that moment

The pain is dulled
Just long enough to temporarily escape
What's really killing me

MY TIME

Madison Celeste James

do you see me here?
I see you
at least I pretend
seeing is believing but believing is seeing
and since you don't believe in me you look straight past me
I feel like Mr. Cellophane but there's no point to singing
cause if you don't see me you sure as hell won't hear me
when all I always wanted was to be heard
and understood
and communication is the bane of my existence
yes I was born in the wrong time
but if my time is one of lies and deception
politicians and supermodels
oppression and pretension
spoons and needles
preservatives and cross-bred fruit
synthesizers and distortion
self-doubt and conceit
parasites and boi-chemical warfare
electric chairs and radiation
diet pills and razor blades
anxiety attacks and shock therapy
plether and nylon
then I dare not claim it as my own
Just leave me with my music
my dance
my love
my truths

my drag queens
my anarchists
my vegans
my hash pipes
my clothes
my scat
my homoerotica
my visions
my fiber arts
my life
my voice
and I will forever be content

PINNED

Jillian Allen

Smear ink/Twist arms/Shatter veins
Pulsing with Pain
Aching and pleading
While choking bloody rain
Dying to cry
But the tears won't come...
Fuck Me
Break Me
Hate Me
Rape Me
Love Me
Taste Me
Destroy Me
Suck down ashes
Vomit up lungs
Bleed salt tears
of pale red pain
I would ask you to kill me...
But I'm already dead.

THE SHIPWRECK

Morgan Anne Wulforst

Mirthless divers ravage
The sunken scene
Of creaking secrets.

Only five feet under,
But do utterly unattainable
To those who seek.

Stumbling
Blindly, the
Dots and rings are

Peeled from their extraneous
Orbs, vying to discover which
They will wish, they

Had not. The pin-pricks
Of their touch bleed the
hallows of the deep.

Yet only the
Sweet bequeaths
Them. Unsatisfied,

They drive to the creamy
Bone to quench their
Insatiable curiosity,

And gorge themselves
On the red insides
Of their prey.

Quickly. They drop
Their claim on the
Organ and scuttle away

Into the hot springs
Of blood and warmth.
My heart leaks.

978-0-595-35486-3
0-595-35486-6